OCEAN MOTHER

Arielle Taitano Lowe

PRAISE FOR OCEAN MOTHER

"With poems like shards of sea glass, Lowe is searching for a home, a mother, a song. A debut full of sea, sky, and promise."

— Julian Aguon, Pulitzer Prize finalist for
"To Hell With Drowning" and author of
No Country for Eight-Spot Butterflies and
The Properties of Perpetual Light

"In this haunting debut collection, Arielle Taitano Lowe sifts through a 'graveyard of Indigenous traditions' to reclaim poem by poem CHamoru culture, and word by word its own language. The author is 'soul fishing.' Readers will be grateful to be invited along."

—Kimberly Blaeser, Wisconsin Poet Laureate 2015-2016
and author of *Ancient Light*

"Born of Lowe's deep guinaiya for her island, her people, and her culture, this book marks the emergence of an important famalao'an voice in CHamoru poetry and in Pacific poetry, one firmly committed to truth-telling and the healing power of our ocean."

—Brandy Nālani McDougall, Hawai'i Poet Laureate 2023-2025
and author of *'Āina Hānau, Birth Lands*

"Arielle Taitano Lowe's first book of verse, *Ocean Mother*, is filled with currents that move like water, crossing bloodlines, seas, timelines, and histories. Lowe's words cast spells of healing stories as traditions realign in these pages. This is a beautiful and powerful book."

—Denise Low, board member of Indigenous Nations Poets
and Kansas Poet Laureate 2007-2009

Ocean Mother

ARIELLE TAITANO LOWE

UNIVERSITY OF GUAM PRESS

PRESS

Published by University of Guam Press
Richard F. Taitano Micronesian Area Research Center (MARC)
303 University Drive, UOG Station
Mangilao, Guam 96923
(671) 735-2153/4

www.uogpress.com

ISBN:
9781935198864 (paperback)
9781935198826 (hardback)
Library of Congress Control Number: 2023951067

Editor: Verna Zafra-Kasala
CHamoru Language Orthography Editor: Anna Marie Arceo
ʻŌlelo Hawaiʻi (Native Hawaiian) Language Orthography Editor: Kamakaʻike Bruecher
Cover and Interior Layout Designer: Ralph Eurich Patacsil
Cover Artist: Ciara Sana

This publication was made possible with support from an Equity in Verse grant from the Poetry Foundation. The Poetry Foundation recognizes the power of words to transform lives and works to amplify poetry and celebrate poets by fostering spaces for all to create, experience, and share poetry.

Note: The author has chosen to follow an older orthography in her spelling of "Chamoru." The word is now spelled "CHamoru" according to the official Guam orthography. Other instances of words that do not follow the official Guam orthography are also intentional and reflect the author's artistic choices.

For you, Chamoritta, with an ocean heart.

FOREWORD

"It is not in words spoken that we have been taught, but rather in the silent teachings of our *Saina*. What we learn is to open ourselves to the 'collective memory' of our People who came before us and help us to move ahead – *I Taotaomo'na*. They show us how to remain in spiritual love and connectedness with each other and our homelands" (C. T. Perez, *Signs of Being*).

CHamoru poetry has existed in its oral form for centuries through lålai and kånta (chant and song), as well as through the oral practice of kåntan CHamorita. The CHamoru people come from a history of poetic orators, a lineage of spoken lines and stanzas, where our ancestors drew connections between themselves and their natural environment, the tåno' (land) and tåsi (ocean), flora and fauna, and spiritual and physical realms. Francisco Garcia, S.J. wrote in his biography of Spanish Jesuit priest Diego Luis de San Vitores that the priest had observed of the CHamoru people in the 1600s: "...[T]hey admire poetry, and consider poets men who work wonders."

In the 1990s, there was a CHamoru renaissance occurring in Guåhan in the midst of land rights struggles, self-determination issues, and the desire for CHamoru language revitalization. Some CHamoru poets were writing and publishing poems related to these CHamoru realities. For example, C. T. Perez, Anne Perez Hattori, Tina DeLisle, Keith Camacho, and Maria Yatar published poems in *Storyboard 5: A Journal of Pacific Imagery* ("Hale yan Ramas Siha"), a creative journal published annually by the University of Guam's Division of English and Applied Linguistics in partnership with the University of Guam Press.

These poets were arguably some of the first to put published CHamoru poetry on the map. At the time, and until about 15 years ago, published CHamoru poetry was not commonly found in Guåhan or anywhere else in the world. Most local people were only familiar with mainstream poetry written by poets they studied in high school American and British literature classes. It was typical to think that poetry was reserved for writers from places and cultures so distant from our own contexts and experiences.

Around 2010, a wave of CHamoru art hit Guåhan's local scene. Much of the visual and literary art that came out during this time was created in response to a proposed U.S. military buildup: the relocation of thousands of U.S. Marines from Okinawa to Guåhan, the construction of live-fire and hand grenade ranges that included a potential firing range at the ancient CHamoru village of Pågat, and a berthing station for a nuclear-powered aircraft carrier. Environmental, cultural, health, and social impacts of the buildup were key concerns for the people of Guåhan and were often the themes of CHamoru artists' — including poets' — work.

Contemporary CHamoru poetry, in both its oral and written forms, is an example of the continuance of traditional practices of poetry, storytelling, and lålai. It has been used as an artform and avenue to tell stories from the CHamoru perspective, convey messages related to CHamoru thoughts and beliefs, inform people about CHamoru experiences, and capture cultural and historical moments or memories. CHamoru poetry has also served as a means of activism, a way for the CHamoru people to express their dissatisfaction with and disappointment in our colonial contexts and to speak against the injustices of our people and our islands.

Because of our colonial context, we in Guåhan are generally ignored by the U.S. military and the greater U.S. government. Our concerns are glossed over, and we are often silenced. For those engaging in the critical work of decolonization, this has allowed us to re-connect with the thoughts and ways of our ancestors and has given us the ability to write and to let our voices be heard, even though politically, this does not typically happen. Poetry creates space and allows us to enact our agency and our voice, without having to seek the approval of the colonial power.

Poetry from CHamoru perspectives also addresses issues of representation. It allows the CHamoru people to write our own stories in our own ways, telling our stories from our perspectives, thus creating avenues to see ourselves in these stories. Gone are the days when the only literature we would read or were exposed to focused on people, places, and experiences that looked nothing like us or that we could not relate to. In the past 15 years alone, the growing literary genre of poetry has been evident in the expanding body of works and of poets, some of which include *Storyboard, Local Voices, Kinalamten gi Pasifiku, Indigenous Literatures of Micronesia, Inside Me an Island* and *A Bell Made of Stones* by Lehua M. Taitano, *An Insider's Voice* by Frederick B. Quinene, *Taimanu na Ini* by Peter R.

Onedera, *The Properties of Perpetual Light* by Julian Aguon, *Dry Nights* by Pep Borja, and now, *Ocean Mother* by Arielle Taitano Lowe, among others.

In line with the growing body of poets and poetry, there has also been a growth in literary groups, the revival of a local publishing press, and course offerings at the University of Guam. The Sinangån-ta Youth Movement (SYM) was created in 2007 by Melvin Won Pat-Borja, Kie Susuico, Fanai Castro, and Jovan Tamayo. SYM focused on spoken word poetry, nurturing and mentoring youth through poetry writing workshops and poetry slam events, which provided opportunities for youth to not only share their poems but also perpetuate the CHamoru practice of oral storytelling. In 2015, the University of Guam Press — a publishing arm of the University of Guam which houses MARC Publications and Taiguini Books — was revived. It has continued to grow since and, in more recent years, has assisted with publishing multiple books of poetry. Ta Tuge' Mo'na — a local literary group formed by the 2016 Festival of the Pacific Arts Literary Arts delegation — published two anthologies, *Local Voices* and *Kinalamten gi Pasifiku*. In 2022-2023, a CHamoru Literature course (taught by Dr. Evelyn Flores) and a CHamoru Poetry course (which I taught) were offered for the first time at the University of Guam.

It is important to note the growth of CHamoru poetry in Guåhan. It was a way for CHamoru ancestors to capture their experiences and tell their stories. Today, while mostly written, it continues to serve a similar purpose. But one must also consider the colonial circumstances experienced by CHamorus and how they shaped the ways in which CHamorus generally accepted not seeing themselves in literature or in the lessons that they were learning in school. These colonial circumstances also contributed to the poor state of the CHamoru language and CHamorus' general lack of knowledge about our language, culture, and history. Poetry has been a way to talk about these experiences, to explore our identities, and to re-connect with ancestors who engaged in this practice.

Ocean Mother by Arielle Lowe serves as a vessel in flight, a paluma (bird) taking us on a special hinanao (journey) which observes and honors the ebbs and flows of the waters of our Ocean and the rootedness and stillness of i tano'. This paluma begins its journey at home ("Origins"), migrates at a particular time of the year, travelling and experiencing different things ("Taking Flight"), and then returns home for rest, re-connection, and rejuvenation ("Returning Home"). Full of beautiful, powerful lines and stories which capture moments, recall memories with elders, and show the struggles of traversing through unpredictable circumstances, this collection consistently reminds us of the power of the wisdom of our ancestors and our elders and the ability of our tåsi and tåno' to nourish us and keep us whole. *Ocean Mother* reveals the intricate and interdependent relationship between paluma and i tano' yan i tasi. None can live fully without the others. Thus, this book serves as a reminder of our interdependent relationships with each other and with our environment and the necessity of deeply caring for and maintaining these relationships in order to thrive in our everyday lives.

In "Origins," Arielle honors and captures the intimate relationship we have with our land and ocean. "Origins" alludes to our roots, the place and people we come from. Arielle tells of her roots and the significance of her relationship to land and ocean through capturing her relationship with her papa, a peskadot (fisherman). Poetry and stories can function as forms of intergenerational healing, and relationships between the past and the present, between manåmko' (elders) and famagu'on (children), can be healed and strengthened through poetry grounded in hinenggen CHamoru (CHamoru beliefs) and inspired by ancestral wisdom.

In "Taking Flight," Arielle takes us on a journey, her poems focusing on various experiences and places outside of Guåhan, such as in Oʻahu and the continental United States. Her work touches on our connections to other Native peoples. Like birds who migrate away from home during certain times of the year, it is as if we are journeying to other places and experiences, connecting with Native siblings, while still rooted in our home and carrying the intention to return.

In "Returning Home," Arielle hones in on issues related to language, culture, and identity. She writes about different cultural practices, including dancing, weaving, and storytelling. She speaks to symptoms of colonial experiences and impacts of militarization, as well as shares stories of original CHamoru place names and kept memories. It is on this part of the journey that we return home to the motherland. Returning home allows us to be re-rooted and re-connected to our ancestors and elders, our culture, our environment, and our purpose. It is here at home where the paluma finds rest and much needed strength to thrive and await the next journey.

As Arielle's former mentor and creative writing teacher, and as a poet, I thought it fitting to end with a poem. Este i rigalu-hu para guiya, my gift for her.

Kalan i paluma gi langhet
      gugupu gi sanhilo' i tasi
      humåhanao gi sanhilo' i tano'

Este i hinanao-mu.

Lao ti hinanao-mu na maisa ha'.
Este i hinanao para i taotao-måmi
yan i tano'-måmi lokkue'.

Esta un hasso' ginen amånu hao.
Esta un tungo' ginen amånu ham.

Pues hånao mo'na, paluma.

Yan i guinaiya-mu put i tano'
i gineggue-mu put i tasi
i inadahi-mu put i taotao-mu

Gumupu

Lumailai

Umaligao

Umeyak

Annai dinanche na tiempo,
annai guaha i lugåt-mu,
pues maila' tåtte fan gi tano'-måmi.

Yan sangåni ham
i ineyak-mu
i tiningo'-mu
i estoriå-mu.

Este i hinanao-mu.

Sangåni ham put i hinanao-mu.

KISHA BORJA-QUICHOCHO-CALVO, Ph.D.
MANGILAO, GUÅHAN

TABLE OF CONTENTS

ORIGINS

TAKING FLIGHT

RETURNING HOME

PREFACE

Ocean Mother is comprised of poetry written between the fall of 2011 and the spring of 2023. The earliest poems in this debut collection came to life while I was between the ages of 17 to 19. They are accompanied by the subtitle *"birthed in ..."* and the year in which they were first written, between 2012 and 2014, marking their emergence during my debut as a youth slam poet.

As a senior at George Washington High School in Mangilao, Guam, I found refuge in my creative writing notebook. I scribbled down freeverse during lessons taught by Dr. Kisha Borja-Quichocho-Calvo, continued writing while on the cracked leather seat of a non-air-conditioned GDOE school bus, and read my poems aloud during "snaps time." The first poems I wrote talked about my cultural identity and the complexities of living in an unincorporated U.S. territory. I also wrote about love, loss, and family, from the perspective of a teenage Chamoru girl in Guam trying to find my place in the community and in the world. My poems were received well by my peers at the time, and my teacher encouraged me to compete in the Sinangån-ta Youth Movement qualifying poetry slam held at the University of Guam Lecture Hall. I placed and went on to compete at the Island Grand Slam Finals at the Tiyan GATE Theater, where I earned a spot on Guam's national youth poetry team. This writing debut happened before I could say the words "colonialism," "patriarchy," or "sovereignty."

As I think about my seventeen-year-old self, the poems gathered here, ultimately, are for her, and others like her. In this collection, I share the transformations in both my writing style and my understanding of the conditions we collectively inherit as Indigenous people. I weave together my personal reflections with the cultural and social, past and present, ecological and intergenerational. This collection captures how my poetry has grown and changed through time, just as I have. Alongside the slam poems of my youth, are poetic prose, map poems, eco-poetry, hydro-poetics, documentary poetry, and form poems (such as the golden shovel), inspired by various writing workshops and courses. Particularly, the time I spent at the Mokulei'a Writers Retreat (2015; 2019), during a poetry manuscript course taught by Susan Schultz at the University of Hawai'i at Mānoa (2020), and attending workshops by Indigenous Nations Poets at the Library of Congress (2022) introduced me to these poetic genres.

Reflecting Indigenous ways of remembering story, I refrain from compiling these poems chronologically. Much like memory cycles, the time, place, and maturity of my voice are woven together throughout the collection, sequenced by theme rather than age. Much like our moon phases, planting seasons, and weaving techniques, I believe that healing and creating are cyclical.

Most importantly, I believe that my intellectual and creative curiosity, love of language, and love for my home islands of Guam and the Northern Marianas, is a profound love and curiosity that I have inherited from my ancestors. They remind me that poetry is an inherently Chamoru expression.

To our youth, I hope this collection can tell you: there is no story you bear that renders you unlovable. We need you, and we need your stories. Truth-telling and showing up for each other is how we will continue to heal ourselves, our bloodlines, our community, and our people. I hope these poems can hold you, as they have held me.

ARIELLE TAITANO LOWE
MANGILAO, GUÅHAN

ORIGINS

OCEAN MAPPING | APAPA

Hu siente i manglo' ginen i tasi, gi iya Apapa.
 I bare myself to the shore of Apapa
  soles of my feet in the coral-born sand,
   ocean water reverberating, deepest resonance binding me to shoreline,
    wave seeping into both sand and skin,
    palms open, facing the sea.
   I pull ocean breeze into my lungs as ancestral breath.
  Månglo', the wind, gently tosses and combs through my hair,
an ocean mother's fingers.

Guåhan
   inward curvature,
  limestone waist
 reef extends once again
outward curve to form nestled bay.

West side, crescent, coral habitat
  rich fishing grounds for mamulan, ålu, and botague.
   coral homes to schools of palakse' of every color swimming in spirals
   håggan surface and gåga glide across
choppy, sapphire blue, white speckled waves and swells.

Feet in the sand of Luminao Reef:
  smooth pieces of shell fizzle upon a bubbling spring.
   Månglo', the wind, brushes across the bridge of my nose,
   around my cheeks, into the strands of my hair.
  gi chepchop unai, the place where the waves tumble and suck up the sand
upon an ever-shifting harbor tide.

The top left crescent peak curves lågu, into Philippine sea
  an upper torso of Apapa:
   Luminao reef to
Urote Point, protruding bottom curve.

Playing in the crescent moon bay, ancestral waters,
Sumai greets us across the waterway:
the view from Luminao, a place of re-membering.
Åcho' tåsi, coral mothers, teach us
through ocean understory
to blossom amongst the coral beds,
steadfast in substrate, and take in the sunlight.

Who will teach us the ways of the ocean
if not our mothers?

Pontan washed ashore,
I am born beached:
sprouted, salt-watered,
Ocean roots into
island.
I have become,
always becoming.
This place will always be,
always be the seed.

I tasi, giya Apapa, ha pulan yu'.
The ocean at Apapa, she raised me,
since five-years-old napping in coral-born sand,
ocean water reverberating,
rocking me against a tidepool cradle,

the sounds: a wavebreak lullaby.

OCEAN NAMES

your dad chose your name

Ariel, after The Little Mermaid
        the girl born
                part-fish,

                who wanted to leave the water,
but I chose the spelling

added an
        -le
                at the end

to make it different
unique

                      when she was little, about five years old
                          she fell asleep in the car

                      at the end of our long work day
                          at the beach in Apra.

                      we always took her with us.
                    the beach was her baby-sitter.

                  you could never get her out of the water.

I taught you how to swim
when you were two years old,

showed you how to plug your nose,
       close your eyes

       and kick your feet.
paddle them like flippers.

by the time you were four
       we could leave you alone

in the reef

       swimming in the sand pocket
by the orange coral head
       for hours

I carried her little body
from the car

to the bathtub
to shower her down,

she pretended to sleep
eyes closed

she stood up-right in the tub
head tilted on her shoulder

your auntie let you jump
        back into the water

                when I wasn't looking
                it pissed me off
                        I already changed you
                into your dry clothes

        we packed everything already

and the harbor gates were closing

                                        when her bathing suit bottom
                                        came off in the shower,

                                                a whole pile of sand
                                                plopped into

                                                        the tub.

                                        she took the beach with her

        We should have named you *Sirena*.

CAPTAIN KERT

compact, rectangular, bright blue
1 gallon Igloo portable cooler,
one-foot deep,
with a handle

nahong
to carry just what you need

black blizzard ice pack
three bottles of water

because it's 90 degrees
at the beach

three aluminum cans of Coke Zero
to keep your teeth from falling out

fanny pack wrapped
around the cooler's trunk

so there's no need
to go digging

U.S. Merchant Mariner Credential License
always renewed on time

fishing knife sheathed
two pairs of work scissors
because you never know

pliers
multi tool

to remove fish hooks and tie lures

tiny black pen
black sharpie

straight to the point
to keep things labeled

super glue
for cracks in the boat
or cuts on the feet

black face covering
to prevent the spread of COVID-19

a small silver key
tied to a string
that way you don't lose it

green dental flosser
for picking at your teeth
just like Nåna Hågat would

Not pictured:

[my father]
in Oakley polarized shades
for seeing fish beneath the surface

Marlboro Green Lights, short pack
for the habit you could never quit

Dallas Cowboys hat
you always wore
faded and weathered from salt water winds,
ocean and sweat.

CHAMAOLI

Birthed in 2014

I notice how I often confuse people because
I am

a white girl eating kådu
a white girl going fishing for tarakitu
a white girl selling atulai at the flea market
a white girl getting an "A" in Chamoru class
a white girl who hates haoles

and

a chamoru girl speaking English
a chamoru girl wearing Hollister
a chamoru girl listening to Sum 41 and Fall Out Boy
a chamoru girl using Mac make-up and brushes
a chamoru girl who loves watching One Tree Hill

a white girl starting to speak Chamoru
a white girl going to nginge' her grandma
a white girl making finadene and kelaguen
a white girl born and raised in Guåhan

a chamoru girl going to University
a chamoru girl with hazel eyes
a chamoru girl dancing the wobble
a chamoru girl with ancestors from England and Germany

Yeah, I am

a chamoru girl eating kådu
a chamoru girl going fishing for tarakitu
a chamoru girl selling atulai at the flea market
a chamoru girl getting an "A" in Chamoru class
a chamoru girl who hates haoles

and

a white girl speaking English
a white girl wearing Hollister
a white girl listening to Sum 41 and Fall Out Boy
a white girl using Mac make-up and brushes
a white girl who loves watching One Tree Hill

a chamoru girl starting to speak Chamoru
a chamoru girl going to nginge' her grandma
a chamoru girl making finadene and kelaguen
a chamoru girl born and raised in Guåhan

a white girl going to University
a white girl with hazel eyes
a white girl dancing the wobble
a white girl with ancestors in England and Germany.

I am a

Chamaoli girl dancing the wobble.
Chamaoli girl dancing the båtso and chåcha.
Chamaoli girl with ancestors from Hågat, Otdot, England, and Germany.
Chamaoli girl born and raised in Guåhan.

CHAMORU KAIKAMAHINE

Mom pulls into the white gravel parking lot
of Barrigada mayor's office
on a Tuesday evening.

Late again.

I step out of her dark blue Toyota 4Runner,
aloha print hula bag
hung on my shoulder.

Inside,
my hand sewn deep purple pā'ū,
matches the bag I carry:

the official color of Kumu's home island of
Kaua'i.

Alongside my pā'ū is a cheap island print sarong
Mom got me at Kmart,
and standard issue, Marianas Handicrafts i'i
tightly stored in empty toilet paper rolls to
keep the fibers straight and sturdy.

Empty paper towel rolls work better,
if you can afford them.

I flop along in my zories
toward our hālau practice stage,
stepping into my pā'ū as I run,
tripping on the skirt
as I flop about the entrance.

Kumu is waiting.
Now I know I need to hurry.

I find my place in line
with the other kaikamāhine.

Our hālau's name is Famagu'on Guåhan,
Chamoru for "Children of Guam,"

which I never understood because our dance teacher is a
Kumu Hula, we don't learn very many Chamoru dances,
and the other dance groups say that we don't do
real Chamoru dances anyway.

Maybe if I joined a real Chamoru dance group,
I would feel a little bit better about having to go
three times a week, plus show.

But here I am, 11 years old,
dancing hula for three years now,
which I don't understand because
I am not Hawaiian.

Our dance shows in Tumon Plaza
leave me vulnerable and bulging
from my two-sizes too small grass skirt
and coconut bra:

all belly and no boobs.

I scratch at my tight garments
before the crowd of Japanese tourists,
convinced my mom's sole purpose is to
embarrass me.

Or worse,
live her life through me.

Between Kumu's knees,
he holds upright
his ipu heke.

It stands gently upon a
protective island print mat,
faded forest green with
white hibiscus flowers.

A fabric of the same print
tightly hugs the neck
of the ipu heke, between
the round top gourd

and the elongated gourd beneath.

Kumu takes this fabric,
wraps it tightly around his wrist,
and firmly pounds his ipu heke on the ground
two times.

His voice fills the amphitheater,
followed by two deep resounding
booms of the ipu heke:
Ho'omākaukau!

Alongside my hula sisters,
I bend my knees, pā'ū skirt moving with me,
elbows up to our sides,
fingertips meet at the chest.

All at once, the sea of purple pā'ū
lowers several inches
closer to the ground.

I respond alongside them,
our voices resound
together as one:

'Ae mākaukau!

DAUGHTER OF DIVORCE

Birthed in 2014

Mom,
you tucked the framed family photos
from our living room
into your luggage,
like a priest tucks prayers into his palms.

The secret you held on your tongue
weighed heavy like our sins
until you confessed that you were leaving us.

I heard the most righteous reasons
for your departure take flight
from your lips.

You made certain I was last to know

that you were moving from Guam to Arizona
a week before my 19th birthday.
That your love for my father vanished from your heart
as quickly as the wrinkles appeared at the corners of your eyes.

You told me divorce was your decision.

In an instant, my thoughts
drowned in memories
of the past 18 years our family spent
breaking and mending.

You and I worked so hard
to become a mother and a daughter
who use cars as confession boxes
and safely keep the secrets and sins we confided in each other
in the confines of our rib cages.

Because even when abuse kept our family captive,
and separation pried us apart,
our family grew stronger
with every domestic fracture in our spines.
Regardless of our struggles,
I thought you showed me what marriage really was,
that marriage vows are thicker than blood.

You told me that children
are walking manifestations
of love between two human beings,
but Mom, if that's true,
if my parents don't love each other,
what does that make me?

The day your divorce
was printed and notarized,
it felt like the 23 chromosomes I inherited from you
dissolved from my blood cells and divorced from my bloodline.

Now, you have another man's daughter
to raise in Arizona, and I've become
an obsolete prototype on your shelf of mistakes.
You told me that taking care of her
made you see all the mistakes you made with me.

My heart feels irreparable,
like a marriage certificate
burned into ash.

I am a daughter of divorce,
scientifically known
to be a daughter of depression,

but as hurt as I am, Mom, I understand.
That even adults need second chances.

How you were a flower
that was never able to bloom.

You had my brother and me too early
and the weight of our necessities
made your unbloomed petals
wilt faster than time intended.

Now,
you are growing a new garden
in Arizona,
full of strawberries and cacti.

And for the first time,
I see you smiling
even brighter than Arizona's desert sunrise.

But your old garden
in my front yard withers,
where you've left me.

A solitary red hibiscus
with petals as soft as your smile,
facing the horizon for your return.

I am growing
in your wilted
old
garden.

Chin proud and back straight like you taught me.

Where you've abandoned me
to bloom without you.

DISATENTA

Birthed in 2012

Young women
who can't keep their mouths shut
and legs closed
are called,

Disatenta.

Disatenta, meaning disrespectful,
the Chamoru word for young ladies
who bring shame to their elders.

Disatenta.

Disrespectful witches.
A word to describe young women
who are uncertain, angry, or lost.

My role as a young woman,
never had a concrete definition.
I feel like I am being diagnosed
with a condition depicted in contradictions.

Before crosses, before flags,
I came from women,
who led as chiefs,
taught our daughters and sons
to fish and weave.

Our women burned with a passion
and rage so deep,
that we would set huts
of the men who betrayed us
on fire.

Our family roots were intertwined,
linked so tightly,
that our brothers were
right beside us,
feeding the flames.

But in this cage
called patriarchy,
we shame our women,
for having a voice,
and longing to be held.

Why are we in cages?
Why are we in cages?
Why are we not allowed to sing in our cages?

Our ancestry tells us,
we are strong
and we are necessary,

Colonizers tell us,
we are submissive
and we are silent.

I'm not mamalao to say
that disatenta
is a colonizer's
word.

I'm not mamalao to say
that we come from
matrilineal wisdom,
desire, and rage.

I'm not disatenta to stand my ground
and raise my voice.

I'm not disatenta to make changes in a system
designed to keep me silent.

But if disatenta is what you want to call me,
then Disatenta is who I'll be.

Author's Note: The first version of this poem appeared in the 2012
Guam Island Grand Slam Finals and was hand-scribbled backstage at
the Tiyan GATE Theater.

TALAYERU

I saw the sun rise over the ocean:
my first time
standing on the reef
with my Papa.
My feet upon sand,
rock,
urchins tucked between
crab holes, pånglao pockets
at low tide.
Ipao,
the smell of seaweed
and seasalt,
shore to my back,
barrels of ocean chasing the sky before me.
A quarter mile closer to the horizon,
I watched him watch the waves.
His guagua' hugging his waist
as tightly as a child.
The surf up to our knees,
fighting to make us bend
in reverence
to the taotaomo'na in our waters.
The current
could have pulled us
until our knees kissed coral,
but he taught me how to respect the ocean:
stand firmly
when the surf is rising as quickly as the sun.
And I heard raindrops on the water
with no cloud in the sky.
A downpour of sinkers,
pattering into the ocean,
a ring of woven net

promising her it will be faithful.
His arms painted brown from sunlight,
strong arms,
pulling the talåya
full of sesyon and kichu,
teaching me how to pick them from the net
avoiding the painful sting of their spines.
We went home that day
with his guagua'

half full.

Manahong hit.

He said,
Ocean Mother gave us
all that we needed.

JOHNNY ATULAI

from "Johnny Atulai" in Pacific Daily News, The Guam Daily Post, and Pacific News Center[1]

2012

fisherman John Taitano,
better known as "Johnny Atulai"
says he's retiring

after he was arrested and accused [of]
illegally fishing yesterday

harbor master states
port authority [and]
fishing community

can co-exist in the marina.

atulai, or mackerel, pile up in a trash bin

Port Authority of Guam
remove the fish from nets

belonging to fisherman
Johnny "Atulai" Taitano

Hagåtña Boat Basin

Johnny Atulai and his group of friends
spotted a school of atulai in the area

---

1 See Endnotes

700 pounds of atulai
scad mackerel
confiscated

why something
so important to Chamorro culture
deemed illegal?

port officials had been trying
to clean the two nets that were filled with fish
more than two hours
still cleaning it

Taitano
offered to help clean the nets
so it could take way less time,

port officials said
against protocol

1977 law restricting
the use of fishing nets
at the boat basin
Sen. Benigo Palomo

1982 Sen. Tommy Tanaka
changed the law
to allow cast nets
other restrictions in place

Taitano

      fishing for   67 years

before there was a boat basin

     had to change his techniques as the rules have changed

                             "net fishing [...]
                             surround nets
                     prohibited by law [...]
                  that's all there is to it"

                             only an issue
              when the atulai are running
         July and November each year

              Atulai season

catches atulai using a net
called a chenchulu
which can catch a ton of fish
or more

[or] using a tekken
a net that is
six feet deep

atulai are bait fish
but   at Guam's shores
         considered a delicacy

                 he recently acquired a 600-foot-long net
                     which cost $32,000

         his first arrest for alleged fishing violations
          in 1971, after he returned from Vietnam

2018

Johnny "Atulai" Taitano
        just wants to fish.

In the last 60 years,
he's been arrested
        38 times.

                "No one has a problem with
                Chamoru fishing rights"
                Sen. Wil Castro, R-Barrigada

another run-in
        Port Authority of Guam police.

"They're confiscating
the fish, the nets, the boats.
        It's sad. I'm a fisherman."

Taitano, 73
nickname "Johnny Atulai"

                concerned that large amounts of fish
                being caught, using non-traditional
                fishing methods then sold
                complaints by other fishermen
                "envious of his ability [and]
                experience"

"costly fishing gear"

not concerned about overfishing
of atulai – an abundant species

Manny Duenas, president of the
Guam Fishermen's Cooperative Association

"It doesn't make sense
that fishermen using nets are prohibited
by Guam law from selling their catch."

Law states,
fish cannot be marketed
can be shared with family [and]
community for purposes of
home consumption

Duenas said,
island's fishing tradition
is under attack.

"I feel for these fishermen.
Nobody cares about them.
They're trying to get rid of the fishermen."

Guam law [says]
nets can be used to catch fish,
but fish taken by net
for subsistence only

cannot be sold

local farmers and artists not
prohibited from selling their work,
but net fishermen
prohibited from selling their catch

without fishermen like Taitano
many residents would not have
access to atulai

"How are Tan Maria and Tun Jose,
in Dededo and Yigo,
going to eat atulai?"

unless they try to catch it themselves

"After Johnny is dead and gone,
there will be no more atulai for the people of Guam,
because nobody knows how to catch."

> "These guys are all talk,"
> Taitano said.
> "The politicians, they only come
> and push and shove when their ass
> is in the corner, not mine."

SOUL FISHING

Birthed in 2013

You said to me,
Baby, write me a poem about peace.
Something that will bring me to tears.

On late nights like this,
your voice slurs
and stories spill
onto the table,

and I swear I hear
the hum of old rifles
firing.

The walls of our home
transform into jungle,
and you're a young Chamoru boy
once again,

on the front lines of
America's war
in Vietnam.

You were a Navy Corpsman.

At age 17, they called you
Doc.

You took cover from bullets,
placed pressure on wounds,
cauterized and stitched skin.

You were the island boy
who taught starving U.S. Marines
how to pick and peel
mangoes from trees.

You were pattera to
village mothers
birthing babies.

Papa,
I always wanted to be
brave like you.

Night after night,
I sat, at age 17, and you 63,
at your outdoor coffee table,
cigarette in hand.

I would swat away the smoke
and drink in your stories.

Papa,
my bare feet were still tender.
I wasn't ready to walk
a mile in your shoes.

During the war,

you found
what remained
of your best friend
in a tree.

Clumps of his butchered
flesh

hung
from branches

like mangoes.

I watched you
try to numb the flashbacks
with alcohol.

With a 12-pack catalyst of abuse,
you shot curses from your tongue
like bullets,

except we became the casualties:

our family has been bleeding
for decades

in the aftermath.

Papa, I would do anything
to set you free from
Post-Traumatic Stress Disorder (PTSD).

Papa,
ten years later,
I don't sit at your table,
but I carry you with me.

I write this poem
for our generational
healing.

You told me,
Baby write me a poem about peace.

This poem is for you.
See Papa, you're not just a Corpsman,
you're a legendary local fisherman.

You're Johnny Atulai
catching legendary schools of guihan.

Today, you stitch nets,
doctor plants in your garden,
share stories and water seeds.

Sea salt and soil
cleanse your tainted memories.

You said

Baby, don't come to me
with a penny in your pocket,
because I've got a hundred dollars
worth of experience.

Papa,
whether you're a Corpsman or a fisherman,
I have 28 years worth of loving you,
and no memory of war could sever
how proud I am to be a part of you.

My apatte is a gånta of strength,
and my voice, like yours, rings loud
through the silence.

Thank you, for taking me

soul fishing.

TAKING FLIGHT

INTROSPECTION

Mom taught me the best way
to heal a wound is from the inside out.

I take a walk inside myself,
into the chambers of my heart.
I drag the palm of my hand
across its red, pulsating walls.

The scar tissue, textured ripples,
open up to what lies beneath.

A resounding echo.
A reopening of wounds for cleansing.

Just one transformation
of many.

But will I allow myself to speak
what rises to the surface?

WEAVING BLOODLINES

after the wreckage
I drift, buoyant,

trench deep
in memory.

I am once again
age sixteen,

daughter thrown out to sea:

    jetsam   raked   across   the   reef.

CPS
social workers

sift
through the carnage

excavate stories

beneath waves of welts,
scratches, and bruising.

my neck,
an anthology.

after my mother
and my mother's mother

inherit

the drowning –

BLOODLINES AT SEA

I leave Guåhan
age twenty-six

ripped from the coral bed

as bloodlines
thin from departure.

It's been three years
since I spoke to my mother.

In my mother's absence,
a pelagic echo

pulls me from the
O'ahu shoreline

out to sea.

Instead,
Ocean Mother,
holds me.

Beneath each rock
in the trench

of my
body,

she soothes every
tainted thing.

She whispers,

the bloodlines
we inherit

are ours to weave.

WEAVING DAY

It's maintenance day
at Kuykendall.

I see a pile of coconut tree branches,
stacked and stacked on the sidewalk,
torn from the base of their mother rib.

Five piles, stacked five fronds upwards.
Each frond close to ten feet long,
topped with little
coconut flowers

blossoming, blooming
thick with honey bees
circling, resting, consuming sweet
coconut nectar.

A bouquet of daddek
fans out atop the piles,
I reach out and touch
the bottom of the stack

and grab hold of the bayak
Tug, gently. Softly shake
here and there.

Pull, nice and smooth, like a jenga block,
so as not to disturb the bees.

Carrying two fronds upon my back,
I make my way to the grassy calm
beside the Mānoa stream.

I look up between the leaves of the dokdok tree,
spaces between, slivers of sky.
Kahaukani rocks the branches
to an ebb and flow,
as I sit beside the Mānoa stream.

Holding the coconut fronds,
I observe the health of each leaf:
matured and bright yellow nuhot,
deep, luscious, forest green.

I count,
  two ...
    four ...
      sixteen ...

hold the knife and cut
into the base of the frond,
peel back the strip of leaves,
away from the stalk,
rest it on my lap.

Gather and roll the stripped base
into the brim of a hat.

Tie and tug.

I fold, and weave, and tug, each row.
Over, under, over, under.
I tighten, I fasten,
until the hat is complete.

KEANU STREET

A year since departing
Guåhan for Oʻahu
and I've moved from Mānoa valley
to Keanu Street next to Waialae Ave.
Jogging up 10th takes me into
Pālolo.
I usually rest at
Ke Kula Kaiapuni ʻo Ānuenue,
stretching at the top of the hill.
I return facing the ocean:
her body framed by the valley's
angled mountainsides,
pointing beyond the town skyline
interrupting

the blue intimacy
of sea and sky.

AWĀWAMALU

O'ahu (2020)

Dive into a calm between
wavebreaks

whitewash dissipates

dreaming and twisting through the tide
unspent

tumbled by a wave
            yanked upwards

swimsuit to ankles
            somersault in a washing machine

plunge and hold

stillness in thrashing

choking on salt water

emerge

surface gasping

wade to shore

waves kiss ankles

observation:

Still here.

Still breathing.

Author's Note: I wrote this poem after emerging from a swim at Awāwamalu, referred to by settlers as "Sandy Beach Park," one of the most dangerous shorebreaks in Oʻahu. Mahalo to Kamakaʻike Bruecher for this experience and to Kainoa Keanaaina for sharing the inoa of this ʻāina.

BIG MAN, LITTLE LAMB

Ubud, Bali (2015)

Wenten says
Bamboo symbolizes people.

Pak says
Rice symbolizes God.

And the cicadas keep crying.

Tutut dances.
Dea dances.
Pung dances.
And the orchestra keeps chiming.

Big man
Little lamb.
Big man
Little lamb.
How much blood is spilled in the name of man?

Big man
Little lamb.
Big man
Little lamb.
How much blood is saved in the name of man?

Wenten cries.
Ibu cries.
Pande cries.
And the cicadas keep crying.

Cicadas cry louder than we can.
Louder than a Big Man.
Louder than a Little Lamb.

The people keep climbing.
The orchestra keeps chiming.
And the bamboo keeps bending.

Wenten says
God is both male and female.

Dea keeps dancing.
Ibu keeps climbing.

And the rice keeps growing.

SHE DOES NOT KNOW
THE RIVER'S NAME

Amarillo, Texas (2019)

Handgun lowered,
she draws in a labored breath
in the cold,

her gaze floating across
cracked mud disrupted by desert brush.

She was from Guam.
He brought her to Amarillo.

Seven of them line up to shoot,
including a six-year-old with a BB gun.

The flat landscape is
disrupted only by the gentle flow

of a shallow river,
gray and clear.

She does not know the river's name.

She stands parallel to the targets
and riverscape before her:

a Barreta M9 in her hands.

Because what girlfriend wouldn't follow
her boyfriend and his friends
to shoot firearms
in thirty degree weather
on a Saturday morning?

Filled aerosol cans of Febreze,
cans of diet coke, their twelve-pack cardboard boxes too,

stand upright, single file,
along the river bank.

She looks across the water from where she stands,
and beams at a towering wall of stones and earth,

high enough for her to wonder
who first climbed upon its perch?
who calls this place home?

He says,

if you graze the air freshener
cans and they fall over,

aim for the middle to watch them
burst open,

To her left and right, shots begin to fire.

Bullets pierce the river's surface,
burst canisters,

chemicals hissing into the air, earth, and water,
and she does not know

how the river keeps
from splitting open.

OF EARTH, TERRAFORMING

A Golden Shovel after Vivian Faith Prescott's "šlahta – Rainy, wet snow or sleet"

Homer, Alaska (2022)

I rest on Tugghet's shore listening
to singing winds as chapters close.
Glaciers puncture the skyline, edging me to
set my eyes on Something Bigger. That
ribbons of twisted kelp, too, uproot from their old
holdfasts and succumb to the currents and crashing shorebreak. A hymn
of seabirds lifts all within me. I am of earth,
terraforming. A granddaughter enchanted
like ancestors before me, who shapeshifted from ocean depths, as
the first human beings. This juncture a
gathering place of elements at midday:
humbled bystander, I succumb to the meeting of sky and the singing of squall.

Author's Note: "Tuggeht is the Dena'ina name for the place also known as Bishop's Beach . . . Homer today occupies unceded Indigenous lands . . . " From Bunnell Street Arts Center, "Tuyanitun: Tugghet, Public Art Sculpture."

WE DANCED WITH JOY HARJO

Native cousins in
native drip,

we danced with
Joy Harjo

on the Library of Congress
steps.

Strobe lights flickered
across the Capitol dome at dusk,

as all 19 of us:

Chamoru
Anishinaabe
Mvskoke
Denai'aina
Kanaka 'Ōiwi
Western Shoshone
Sāmoan
Oneida
Diné
Eastern Band Cherokee
Lummi
Laguna Pueblo
Tongva / Luiseño
Chicana

We danced with Joy
to the Cupid Shuffle

the Cha Cha Slide
and the Twist.

Our ancestors danced, too,
with us. Round and round

in circles,
to Footloose, September,

Shake It Off, and
It was All a Dream.

If you traced our roots
from continents

to oceans
to islands

you would see how native kinship
is an aerial weave:

Together, we have always been dancing.

ORALITY WILL NOT BE CANONIZED
After Michael Lujan Bevacqua's "The Revolution Will Not Be Haolified"

I sat in a room of Native academics
and saw publications weighed more
than genealogies of survival

and if publication means sharpening
my tongue into a capitalist's pen, then my
orality will not be canonized.

I read my poem to my Papa once.
he shrugged and asked
well how much fish can you catch with it?
his orality will not be canonized.

my abuser's name was published
beside mine once, and that's when I knew
my orality will not be canonized.

I conversed in Chamoru with a congressman
at the Library of Congress in D.C. once.
my grandma shrugged at the story, unimpressed
her orality will not be canonized.

I've witnessed spoken word poets
tossed to the side,
local poets demarcated as juvenile,
and that's when I suspected
our orality will not be canonized.

after all, why fight to make an institution
value, what it's never had to fight for?
and why fight the skinfolk,
with a pair of white man's eyes?

Our orality will not be canonized.

RETURNING HOME

TRONGKON NUNU

Birthed in 2014

Si Nanå-hu biha, ti komprendi yu',
annai kumuekuentos gi fino'
        English.

If I speak in English,
my great grandmother can't understand
what I'm saying.

Her native language,
My native language,
is rooted in this land,
just like the banyan trees,

i trongkon nunu,
connects us to our ancestors,

i taotaomo'na,
the first Chamoru people.

And through
invasion after invasion:
conquered by Spain,
taken by America,
occupied by Japan,

waves of genocide,
colonization,
and imperialist policies,
have tried to cut out our native tongues and
uproot our ancestry.

Spanish and Japanese invasions couldn't
eradicate our birdsong.

But today,
back in U.S. hands,
re-occupied by America since 1944,

in my generation,
we are told as often as the ring of school bells,
that
i fino'-ta,
our Chamoru language is disappearing,
dying,
like the absence of birdsong
in our trees.

Decaying
like a
trongkon nunu
slowly rotting with disease.

On our island, English was
forced upon my grandparents.

My grandma tells me
how she was punished for
speaking Chamoru in elementary school.
I wonder if she knew
an English-Only Policy
would spread from the school hallways,
into the school bus,
into our home.

In my family
I come from a second generation of Chamorus
whose first and often only language is English.
In just two generations
our island let this tongue take hold.

Wake up!
English may be beautiful in its own right,
but it isn't native to this land.

I've been pushing through the leaves of books
and digging through the roots of my family,
trying to nurture a language
my grandmothers couldn't pass down to me.

And my roots have led me to them.
My grandmothers taught me
what good soil looks like.
That learning
Chamoru
is as easy as asking them questions.

I can't deny
that language revitalization
blossoms from my tongue.
Buds of banyan flowers
waiting to burst as red
as my grandmothers' achiote-stained hands.

Sen gef pa'go i fino'-ta.
Our language is so beautiful.
My generation may not be flourishing with fluent speakers,
but like my grandmothers say,
we are made of good soil.

Ti siña fumino' yu' prifekto
lao bai hu chagi kada diha para i lina'lå'-hu.
I may not speak perfectly
but I will practice each day,
and pass on what I can.

           Dumodokko' i simiya   gi pecho-ku.
      The seed in my   chest is growing
          with the strength   of my ancestors.

           Dumodokko' i hale   gi simiya,
        anai kumuekuentos yu' gi fino' Chamoru.

Roots burst   from this seed
with each Chamoru word   I speak.

Dumådangkolo i ramas   gi trongkon kanai-hu
          yan gi petnå-ku.
                    The branches are growing inside my limbs.

          Ha chalalapon i hale nunu   gi tataotao-hu.
                    The banyan roots are spreading through my body.

I metgot na håle nunu siña ha pokka' i simento.

The strongest banyan roots can crack colonial cement.

Teniki mayamak i simento,

annai kumahuhulo' i hale manantigu.

This colonial foundation

will crumble,

as the roots of our

ancestors

rise.

COUSIN-GANG

we chase the Miller Lite we siphoned into cans of Pepsi
with Uncle Ron's shrimp patties.

cousin-gang, we patrolled the Tiyan streets on New Year's Eve,
skin sticky with sweat, fingers sticky with Chamoru barbecue

and too much lumpia sauce,
styrofoam fiesta plates filled to the brim

soggy and forgotten on the sidewalk.

we talk story while the adults
empty their beer cans

beneath the canopy
behind grandma's house.

within earshot of Chamoru music blasting
we climb up and over the bus stop walls

swing from the concrete pillars
next to abandoned rusted cars

and splay our bodies
out on the asphalt.

defying the weight
of generations,

with belly-laughter
we pierce the night sky

like fireworks.

HEALING BLOODLINES

cousins-born-sisters / I smoke my first cig with Rae / inside the abandoned house at the end of 2nd street / I swiped a pack of Virginia Slim Lights off a friend at Rios / what my mom smoked when she was my age /

Rae in 9th grade / me in 8th / she brought the lighter / after our first few puffs we / joke that our moms all made a pregnancy pact / after all, they had our brothers at age 14, 16, 18 / our bodies were starting to look sottera / and our parents gave us looks / like we were doomed to follow in their footsteps /

she holds out the cig / barely burned through /
indifferent / she shakes her head and kills it / on the empty shell of a windowsill /
she says – *let's go* / grabs the full pack and throws it into the jungle of tangantångan trees /
this shit ain't that fucking cool anyways.

DECOLONIAL LOVE

My body

Has

Resisted

Offers of love

Incapable

Of tracing

Ancestral strength

Along

My

Spine

THE WEAVERS WERE THE FIRST TO KNOW

The invasion came like a whisper,
and the leaves changed shapes,
and the niyok grew sick.

Coconut trees,
our culture's tree of life,
dying slowly
as invasive beetles
eat their hearts
like world powers
devour islands.

Weavers hold culture in their
palms,
weave tradition into their families, tuck young palms
into their fingers,
mold them into
entities.

But now,
our culture's tree of life
has grown ill from
foreign settlement.

Palms severed,
bent like a salute
the way Chamorus are cut like cards and
dealt in front lines of American wars.

The weavers were the first to know

that our niyok are
sick,
in need of healing.

The same way our island is
sick,
in need of healing.

I've taken up the craft,
so I can weave
traditions
into the palms of my children.
I can only hope that when I master it,

palms will remain
for them

to weave into our future.

DANCE

Birthed in 2013

Dances perpetuate our culture.
Our body movements tell our history,
but 500 years of colonization
paralyzed our native form of storytelling.

Today, I am one of many
hollywood-Polynesian show girls
who sells lies in the form of body language.

My smile is the welcome mat
to an exotic paradise.

As dancers we take the Chamoru greeting, "Håfa
Adai,"
and sell it with our voices:

　　　"Haa-faa adayyyy!"

We represent Guåhan's women
in a dance show that's only 12% indigenous,
but the tourists don't know that.

The audience listens to Polynesian melodies
with Chamoru lyrics woven into them.

Our bodies are covered
with foreign te manu feathers
while the leaves of our local coconut trees,
our trongkon niyok,
silently watch from their branches.

We entice with the hands of hula
and tease with the hips of Tahiti,
and like birds, we scream,
to make our show exciting,

as if our native tongues,
weren't breathtaking enough.

The tourists perceive this as genuine,
and we perpetuate the lie.

This once sacred village, Tomhom,
now called pleasure island,
is a graveyard of Indigenous traditions.

But the tourists cheer for us
for the moving postcards
that stage imitations of culture.

The crowd's applause drowns the truth.
This is not Pacific custom.
            This is a *show*,
sponsored by the suits
who tied traditions to profit.

Businessmen
traded traditional Chamoru dances
for their fake versions of

hula kahiko and hula 'auana of Hawai'i
poi of Aotearoa,
'ōte'a of Tahiti.

We're twirling and
      swaying and dipping
            and shaking and dying
to try and find an escape from our debt
as if we could dance our way into a better economy.

The spirituality of our culture falls as dollar bills
rise like new hotels over buried villages.

Our dances have become
more profitable than meaningful.
These businessmen have turned worship
into entertainment.

It's a shame that we
exploit Pacific culture,
When Indigenous dances
should enrich the livelihood of
the natives they belong to.

Not the pockets of businessmen,
who monopolize the ancient
practices of Pacific peoples
and control them
like cheap commodities.

Representation belongs in native hands,
so our stories can be told beyond promise of income,
our bodies become vessels of truth,
and our dances become bridges to our ancestors.

They are called our Mañaina,
and by respecting them we learn
to respect our island.

The leaves of our trongkon niyok
should no longer watch from their branches.
They should find a home around our women's hips
so the claps of our p a l m s against our skirts
could beat like the p u l s e of our culture.

It may be almost impossible
to revive authentic Chamoru dance,
But we are the pieces that breathe life into it.

Te Manu feathers can soar
away from Chamoru skin
and once again nest on the curves of
their Polynesian women.

The calls of Tahiti can find refuge
curled in the tongues of their people,
while Chamoru chants d a n c e in our mouths.

Our women can hold seashells
in their palms, so the flames of Aotearoa can
burn bright within the hearts of their rightful homeland.

Our dances are as beautiful as our people.

Knowing who we are
has far greater wealth
than any business or tourist attraction.

Owning a business
gives you no right
to own our culture.

HEALING BLOODLINES AT SEA

the last kick back we had was in 2011 / before Kye left for basic right
out of high school / Rae's engagement ring wrapped around her finger
/ Kira growing in Rae's belly / we sat in Rae's black Kia Soul on Marine
Drive / Hand in My Pocket by Alanis Morissette played while we passed
Coffee Beanery in Anigua /

now it's 2023 / Rae and Kye / visit me in Oʻahu / they're 3 kids deep /
their first trip together alone / while Rae's sister in Washington babysits
/ I drive us to North Shore / in Kenton's blue Kia Soul / year 3 into my
PhD with no end in sight / our first time together since we all left home

Kye says / *we had to leave home / we needed space from our family* /
fiesta brawls / brothers' fists / fathers' fists / uncles' fists / sisters' fists
/ mothers' fists / sisters' tears / mothers' tears / grandmothers' tears /
children hiding in bedrooms / children hiding under tables in tears /
the tears our fathers, grandfathers, uncles, and brothers refuse to shed,
but instead pool onto lips that drink until bottles and cans run empty /
how do we come home without the toxicity? /

I mull over the question / as we stop at Waimea and watch the waves /

Rae says / see this line in the sand? / *i'm drawing it and nobody is
fucking crossing* /

I listen to / Rae's stories / Kye's stories / our stories /

echoing /

and ask the sea to hold us.

TYPHOON WOMAN

My mother shape-shifted
          quicker than the rising tide.

Within two minutes,

          malinao

churned

          and raged

          påkyo.

Typhoon woman,

she ravaged,

          wooden doors splintered,

glass shattered,

          tables smashed.

She kicked in waves,

          small bodies

crumpled,

          metal pipes bent
into spines.

We coughed up water,
        but did not drown.

My brother and I

survivors

of

her storms.

SUMAI

Walks with Grandma
make me feel less

displaced.

Agat is the closest we get
to ancestral waterways.

Grandma says,

"my father Jesus Castro Sablan
was born on Pågan

sailed into Sumai Bay,
traded copra,

grew mango trees,
taro, and banana,

rode karabao
into the låncho

planted seedlings in their hoofprints"

[they took all the land, the americans]

"I used to take the kids hiking into Seya'
Let me take you to Nimitz Beach and show you
the Kamachili tree.

Yeah, we have some activist characters
making their stand outside the Navy gate,
but I better not ever catch you protesting."

[they took all the land, the americans
but Nåna said, ti mamaigo si yu'os]

I look up a map on Google
where Grandma says the rows of mango trees
used to be. Where Great-Grandpa Jesus
and Nåna Maria's farmland used to be.

/ displacement sounds like /

t.stell newman visitor center
navy family housing office
navy laundry
national war dog cemetery
charles king fitness center
nex gas station
orote point bowling lanes
navy gateway inns & suites
gab gab beach
orote ecological reserve area
spanish steps

/ memory sounds like /

Sumay Drive
Sumay Pub & Grill
Sumay Cove Marina
Sumay Cemetery

the land where Nåna and Tåta planted and fished
that no longer belongs to us

[they took all the land, the americans
but Nåna said, ti mamaigo si yu'os
god isn't sleeping. she let it be]

ONE DAY OUR BODIES WILL TRULY BE FREE

Hagå-hu,
your body is an island.
Trace its belonging
in this archipelago:

Guåhan,
southernmost of
fifteen sisters,
Låguas yan Gåni.

Your grandmother's
and great grandmother's
and great great grandmother's home.

I tano'-ta i tataotao-mu.
The land is your body.

I tasi i hagå-mu.
The ocean is your blood.

Papangpang lina'la' i kurason-mu ginen i aire.
The air beats life into your heart.

Pues tungo' este hagå-hu,
so know this.

When they come for your body,
extract limestone forest like harvesting organs,
pour toxins into our ocean like poison into your blood-
stream,
carve out lifeblood coral gardens like a uterine invasion
until all that is left are your bones,

I will stand here, resisting,

so that there will always be
an abundance of kåna for you to inherit.

Sumai. Apapa.
Pågan. Litekyan.

They'll never take away your genealogy.
They'll never take away your name.

An archipelago of ocean,
fifteen sisters reunited,
i taotao tåno',
sovereign —

Our islands are your body.
They will be your daughter's body,
and your daughter's daughter's body.

One day our bodies will truly be free.

SWEETEST MANGOES OF JUNE
A Golden Shovel after Casandra López's "Hottest June"

I long for the rooftopping
of Agat mango trees, nesting myself
in clusters of ripened sunset teardrops. Fruiting myself into
a body of canopy stretched and bearing the
bounty, the abundance, the outstretched arms
of leaves. I long for the gathering of
village streets: vendors lined along the
Agat shoreline. The hottest
of Guåhan days, thirst quenched by sweetest mangoes of June.

BIRTHING BLOODLINES

my brother, Jon-jon, and I share stories over the dining table / Thanksgiving / six-year-old niece Railey and two-year-old nephew Hurley dance to B.T.S. in front of the TV / their mom and my sister-in-law, Aya, plates homemade cherry cake with chocolate glaze / we sip on whiskey as the kids spin and dance in circles /

brother shares stories / i share stories / our bloodlines bloom / sibling memory / the garden we were raised in / hibiscus buds unfurling into scar tissue / dark veins stretching across crimson petals / like a swollen cheek from a fist that bloomed / stamen dripping / like a trail of blood from a child's ear / scratches across a child's neck / the stories age, purple / wilted from time that turns bruises into memory

railey says / *nåna used to hit you and daddy / how did you feel? / are you okay?*

I reply / *it's okay baby / it made me feel sad / but your daddy and I don't allow that any more*

our bloodlines resonate /
in this new garden
we have planted

OCEAN MOTHER

Ocean Mother

    knows the currents

        who carved my name.

Calling me from

    matrilineal

        depths,

she beckons me into her

t a l å y a:

    strands of sunlight

        dance across her skin.

Each ripple a reflection
    I trace,

    touch
to fingertips.

        Wrapped in the tropic

        warmth

of my birth

I sink myself

    into her soft
rocking
    waves,

returning home.

ENDNOTES

"Johnny Atulai" is a found poem. According to the Academy of American Poets, "found poems take existing texts and refashion them, reorder them, and present them as poems. The literary equivalent of a collage, found poetry is often made from newspaper articles, street signs, graffiti, speeches, letters, or even other poems."

Lines from this poem are taken from seven different sources in the forms of news articles, spanning across major Guam news outlets *Pacific Daily News, The Guam Daily Post,* and Pacific News Center.

"Johnny Atulai" Bibliography
(numbers in parentheses reflect location of the quote in the poem by stanza number)

Pacific News Center. " 'Johnny Atulai' Taitano Arrested For Illegal Fishing; Questions Port Enforcement Policies." March 5, 2012.

2012 . . . fisherman John Taitano, better known as "Johnny Atulai"says [he's] . . . retiring after he was arrested and accused [of] illegally fishing yesterday (1-3) . . . harbor master . . . [states port authority and] . . . fishing community can co-exist in the marinas (4-5)

Cruz, Rick. "Fisherman Caught Catching Atulai in Boat Basin." Pacific Daily News. July 12, 2018.

atulai, or mackerel, pile up in a trash bin . . . Port Authority of Guam
remove the fish from nets . . . belonging to fisherman Johnny "Atulai" Taitano (6-8)

Sablan, Jerick. "700 Pounds of Atulai Confiscated." Pacific Daily News. July 12, 2018.

700 pounds of atulai scad mackerel confiscated (11) . . . Johnny Atulai and his group of friends spotted a school of atulai in the area (10) . . . Taitano questioned why something so important to Chamorro

culture like fishing would be deemed illegal (12) . . . The Port officials had been trying to clean the two nets that were filled with fish and even after more than two hours were still cleaning it (13) . . . Taitano said the group offered to help clean the nets so it could take way less time (14) but the Port officials said it was against protocol . . . (15)

Limtiaco, Steve. "Port: 'Johnny Atulai' Had Earlier Run-In Over Nets at Boat Basin." Pacific Daily News July 15, 2018.

1977 Law restricting the use of fishing nets at the boat basin Sen. Benigo Palomo (16) . . . 1982 Sen. Tommy Tanaka changed the law to allow cast nets other restrictions in place (17) . . . Taitano . . . fishing for 67 years . . . before there was a boat basin . . . changed his techniques as the rules have changed (18) . . . "net fishing, surround nets prohibited by law that's all there is to it," (19) Duenas said . . . only an issue when the atulai are running (20) . . . using a tekken . . . a net that is six feet deep (23) . . . he recently acquired a 600-foot-long net which cost $32,000 (25) . . . his first arrest for alleged fishing violations in 1971, after he returned from Vietnam (26) . . . envious of his ability (35) . . . costly fishing gear . . . (36)

July and November each year (20) . . . catches atulai using a net called a chenchulu which can catch a ton of fish or more (21) . . . atulai are bait fish but at Guam's shores . . . considered a delicacy (22) . . . "No one has a problem with Chamoru fishing rights" Sen. Wil Castro, R-Barrigada (28) . . . concerned that large amounts of fish being caught, using non-traditional fishing methods then sold (32) . . . "I cannot stand on that side. I cannot turn a blind eye. To people selling it." (38)

Taitano, 73 . . . nickname . . . "Johnny Atulai" (31) . . . not concerned about overfishing of atulai – an abundant species (37)

Limtiaco, Steve. "Head of Local Fishing Organization Questions Fishing Laws." Pacific Daily News. July 16, 2018.

"It doesn't make sense that fishermen using nets are prohibited by Guam law from selling their catch" (40) . . . Duenas said, . . . island's fishing tradition is under attack. (42) "I feel for these fishermen. Nobody cares about them. They're trying to get rid of the fishermen." (43) . . . Guam law . . . nets can be used to catch fish, but fish taken by net, . . . traditional fishing method, for subsistence only (44) . . . cannot be sold (45) . . . local farmers and artists not . . . prohibited from selling their work, . . . but net fishermen . . . prohibited from selling their catch (46) . . . without fishermen like Taitano many residents would not have access to atulai (47) . . . "How are Tan Maria and Tun Jose, in Dededo and Yigo, going to eat atulai?" (48) . . . unless they try to catch it themselves (49) "After Johnny is dead and gone, there will be no more atulai for the people of Guam, because nobody knows how to catch" (50).

Keraskes, Dontana. "Fishing Tradition Halted." The Guam Daily Post. July 16, 2018.

"These guys are all talk," Taitano said. "The politicians, they only come and push and shove when their ass is in the corner, not mine." (55)

Aguon, Mindy & Dontana Keraskes. "Fishing Tradition Clashes with Enforcement." The Guam Daily Post. July 13, 2018.

2018 . . . Johnny "Atulai" Taitano just wants to fish . . . In the last 60 years, he's been arrested . . . 38 times (27-29) . . . another run-in . . . Port Authority of Guam police (31) . . . "They're confiscating the fish, the nets, the boats. It's sad. I'm a fisherman"(32).

TRANSLATIONS

CHAMORU

"Ocean Mapping | Apapa"

Hu siente i manglo' ginen i tasi, gi iya Apapa: I feel the wind from the ocean at Apapa

Månglo': wind

Guåhan: Chamoru name for "Guam"

mamulan: skipjack larger than 15 pounds

ålu: barracuda

botague: dolphinfish

palakse': parrotfish

håggan: sea turtle

gåga: flying fish

lågu: seaward

"Ocean Names"

Sirena: Guam's mermaid

"Captain Kert"

nahong: enough; sufficient; satisfied

"Chamaoli"

tarakitu: skipjack

atulai: big-eyed scad, mackerel

nginge': to smell an elder's hand as a sign of respect and to breathe in their wisdom

finadene: famous Chamoru dipping sauce consisting of lemon juice, hot pepper, onions, and salt

kelaguen: Chamoru dish made by finely chopping meat, fish, or poultry and soaking in lemon juice, hot pepper, onions, and salt

båtso: Chamoru dance from the Spanish colonial era; dancers are usually adorned in ruffled mestisa dresses (for women) or Sunday's best button-down shirts and dress shoes (for men)

chåcha: Chamoru adaptation of the Spanish cha cha dance

"Chamoru Kaikamahine"

zories: slippers

"Disatenta"

mamalao: a sense of humility; a feeling of shame

"Talayeru"

pånglao: land crab

guagua': woven basket, in this case, used to carry fish caught with talåya

taotaomo'na: literally, "the people in front of us"; ancestors

talåya: cast net

sesyon: rabbitfish

kichu: convict tang, a type of reef fish

manahong hit: we are satisfied; we have enough

"Soul Fishing"

pattera: midwife

guihan: fish

apatte: partition of a catch of fish

gånta: a container, similar to a bucket, used as a form of measurement; usually made by cutting off the top of a laundry soap container

"Weaving Day"

daddek: smallest stage of coconut that comes immediately after coconut flowers

bayak: frond's thick base

dokdok: seeded breadfruit

nuhot: center rib of each palm blade

"Healing Bloodlines"

sottera: womanly, as in the bodily changes from a teenager to young woman

"Dance"

håfa adai: hello

"Typhoon Woman"

malinao: calm waters

påkyo: storm with typhoon force winds

"Sumai"

Nåna: mother (literal), but often used for grandmother or great-grandmother in modern times

"One Day Our Bodies Will Truly Be Free"

hagå-hu: my daughter

Låguas yan Gåni: Islands of Marianas Archipelago

kåna: spiritual power

i taotao tåno': the people of the land

'ŌLELO HAWAI'I (NATIVE HAWAIIAN LANGUAGE)

"Chamoru Kaikamahine"

pā'ū: women's traditional skirt used in hula

kumu: teacher, mentor (status achieved through vigorous training and cultural recognition)

i'i: implements resembling hand tassels used in Tahitian dance

hālau: long house, as for canoes or hula instruction; meeting house

kaikamāhine: girls

kumu hula: highly regarded teacher of hula; status achieved means recognition is given to run your own hālau hula, or hula school

ipu heke: gourd drum with a top section

ho'omākaukau: to make ready, to prepare; here, the kumu asks the dancers if they are ready to begin

'ae mākaukau: yes, I am ready; response to the Kumu

"Weaving Day"

Kahaukani: a wind of Mānoa

"Keanu Street"

Ke Kula Kaiapuni 'o Ānuenue: Native Hawaiian Language Immersion School of Ānuenue

"Awāwamalu"

  inoa: name

'āina: land, earth

ACKNOWLEDGEMENTS

Si yu'os ma'åse to the editors of the following publications, where earlier versions of these poems appeared:

As/Us: A Space for Women of the World, Issue 4, Decolonial Love: "Dance" (2014)

Storyboard 15: A Journal of Pacific Imagery, Issue 15: "Chamaole" and "Talayeru" (2015)

Sinangan i Pachot, Festival of the Pacific Arts: "Trongkon Nunu" (2015)

Local Voices: An Anthology, Festival of the Pacific Arts: "Trongkon Nunu" (2016)

Indigenous Literatures from Micronesia, University of Hawai'i Press: "Dance" (2019)

Unincorporated Magazine, Humanities Guåhan: "One Day Our Bodies Will Truly Be Free" (2021)

Poem-a-Day, Academy of American Poets: "The Weavers were the First to Know" (May 27, 2022)

Indigenous Pacific Islander Eco-Literatures, University of Hawai'i Press: "Trongkon Nunu" (2022)

Under a Warm Green Linden: "Ocean Mother" and "Sweetest Mangoes of June" (2022)

-DANCE-, Indigenous Nations Poets (In-Na-Po): "Sweetest Mangoes of June" and "We Danced with Joy Harjo" (2023)

GUINAIYA YAN INAGRADESI

Mañaina, en na'i yu' i sinangan, guinaiya, yan ånimu gi sanhalom ini. Hu sen agradesi hamyo ni' inayuda put hinanao-hu. Para bai hu hånao ha' mo'na.

Mahalo nui loa e nā akua Hawai'i, for the mana, 'ai, wai, and hale that have nurtured me during my time in Hawai'i. Ko'u hoa, Kainoa Keanaaina and Kamaka'ike Bruecher, my Kanaka 'Ōiwi che'lu siha who have so generously guided me across the pae 'āina: mahalo, mahalo, mahalo.

Amber Mari Word, un na'i yu' pås. Saina ma'åse for teaching me the power of healing, the practice of letting go, and the importance of taking leaps.

Verna Zafra-Kasala, pattera and editor of *Ocean Mother,* my heartfelt gratitude for you in guiding the birth of this debut collection beneath Makahiki rains in O'ahualua and Fañomnakan rays in Guåhan. Nichole "Palao'an Trongko" Quintanilla, my partner-in-rhyme, thank you for holding me through the writing of many of these poems. Dr. Kisha Borja-Quichocho-Calvo, saina ma'åse for believing in my voice and encouraging me to sign up for my very first poetry slam. Rommel Luis Losinio, thank you for empowering me within the shelter of your classroom, through the wisdom of your words, the kindness of your spirit, and your place as my mentor and safe space in my literary journey. Kiana Brown, Kalilinoe Detwiler, Claire Generous, and Ashley Houghton, the valuable feedback you each provided on my manuscript helped this collection grow, and the profound conversations we shared continue to enlighten me.

The Hetricks: my big brother, Jon-jon, sister-in-law, Aya, niece, Railey, nephew, Hurley, and their pup, Chocolat; The Kongs: Mom, Koni, Ka'u, Keynon, Brian, Kelson, Mari, Maka, Soul, Momo, Howl; I am grateful that we are family. Thank you for continuing to be the ones I can turn to when I am in most need.

To my "Grad-Parents" and the Pooty Tang Pod: Joy Loudermelt, Rob Thompson, Merissa Bunton, Kim Maeyama; the Huynhs: Amanda, Minh Đức, Ardin; The Ibraos: Miquela, Aaron, Keola, Makoa; si yu'os ma'åse for extending your loving homes and pleasant company during my transition from Guam to Hawai'i.

Carolyn Siegman, thank you for our long walks in Mānoa, pumpkin shakes, paradigm shifts, Dave Greco references, and runaway Saturdays. Rachael Han, thank you for your intuitive kindness, sleepover shenanigans, and deep belly laughs in Keanu House kitchen. Bartholomew Lujan Perez, thank you for sitting by my side for 8 hours in Guam's Typhoon Mawar Disaster SNAP line, while I finished the final edits of this book, and for every moment I laughed until I could not breathe. Rhia Jimenez Borja, thank you for loving me in all my stages, and experiencing life together beneath the Tiyan rain, jungle gyms, and GWHS trees.

Lauren Aguillard, thank you for loving me on my darkest days, and keeping me company for all of life's challenging and beautiful moments. Elisa Balbuena, thank you for mopping me up off the floor on days when I feel like I have melted into a puddle, and for planting and watering seeds alongside me, near my ancestral land on Lalo street. Isabella Fuller, keep planting and watering those seeds.

Miigwech, Mvto, and Ahxéhee' to Indigenous Nations Poets for the Inaugural Retreat experience in Washington D.C. and Dr. Elise Paschen for the "Freedom in Forms" workshop at the Library of Congress. Chin'an gheli, Storyknife: A Retreat for Women Writers, for the time, space, and nourishment that gave me the space to organize and bring forth this collection.

Special thanks to UOG Press Director Victoria-Lola Leon Guerrero for believing in my book, gently encouraging me to open up poems written in my youth, and for helping me see my manuscript to completion. Thank you, Via De Fant, for being a champion for my collection and helping me envision ways to connect my work to the next generation of writers.

To each guiding hand, kind ear to listen, and warm presence that I am unable to name here: thank you.

Manggafå-hu. Familiå-ku. My family, here in this life and the next: you are everything within me. Everything I am, comes from you. Saina ma'åse for your guidance and wisdom.

To my grandparents, including the star of this collection, Johnny Atulai Taitano, si yu'os ma'åse for sharing your stories, passing down our culture, and being the original sources of inspiration for all of my literary activism.

Kenton Minoru Kong, hu sen agradesi hao, guinaiya-ku, for a healing kind of love. Thank you for asking me to be Mowgli Kong's mama, and for building a safe and loving home for the three of us.

Hu sen guaiya hamyo,
Arielle

Arielle Taitano Lowe is a Chamorrita poet, born and raised in Guam. She grew up swimming with schools of palakse' off the shores of Luminao Reef in Apapa, Piti. Her work has been featured in *Poem-a-Day* by the Academy of American Poets, *Indigenous Pacific Islander Eco-Literatures*, and *Indigenous Literatures from Micronesia*, among others. She now resides in O'ahu, Hawai'i, where she studies intergenerational healing.

Printed in the USA
CPSIA information can be obtained
at www.ICGtesting.com
LVHW081314180524
780605LV00007B/811